What Can I Do Today?

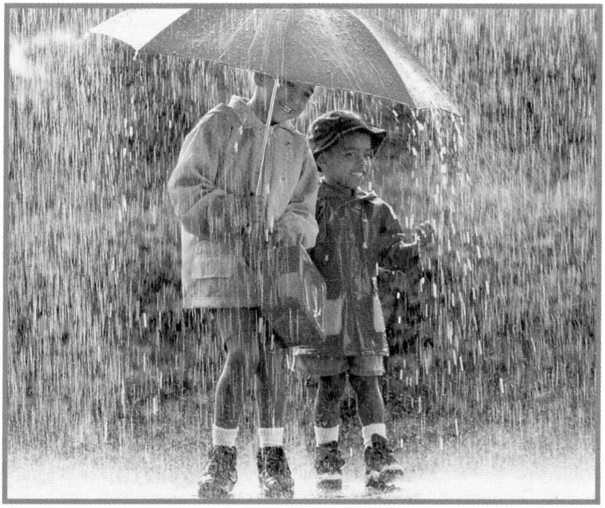

Rose Lorenzo

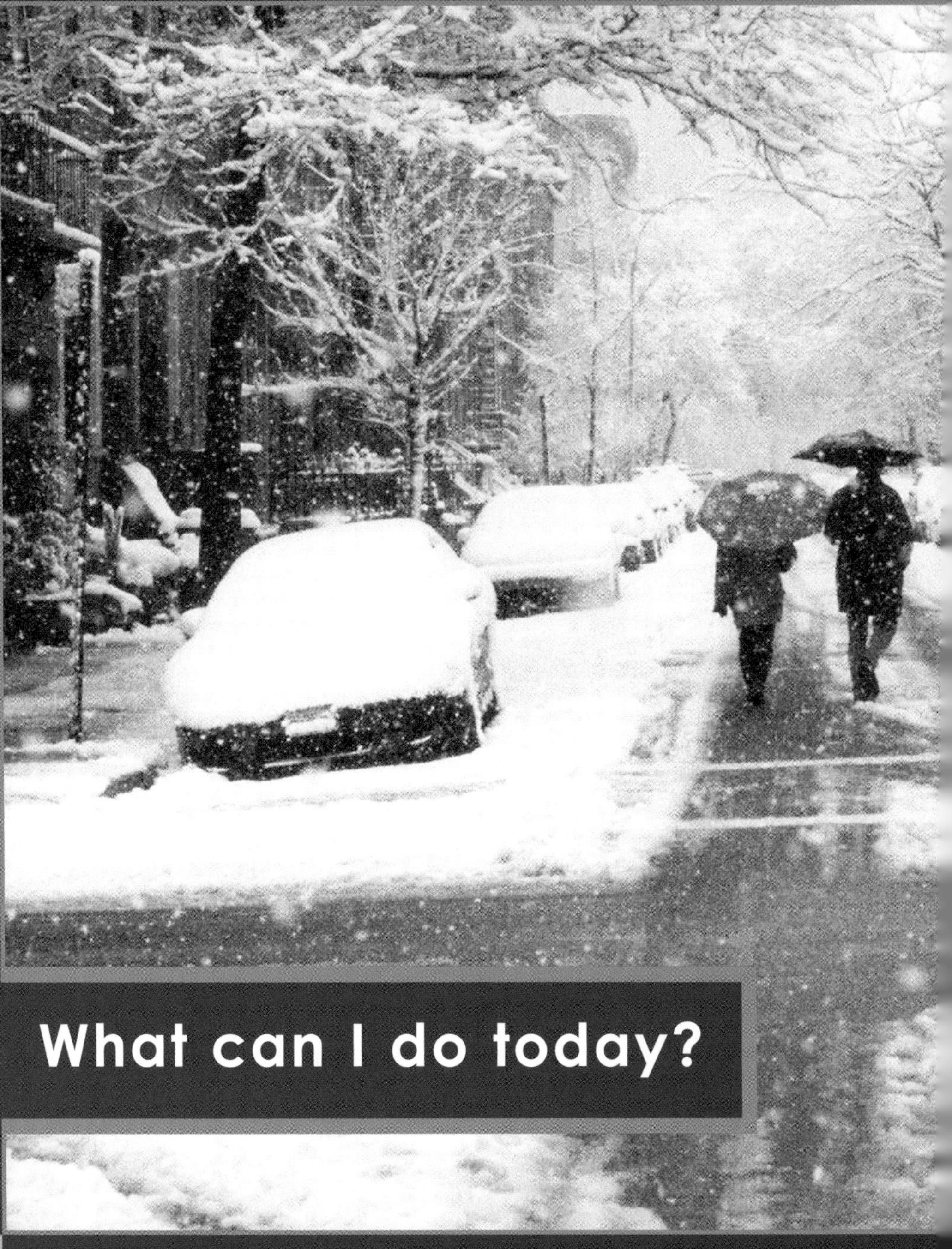

What can I do today?

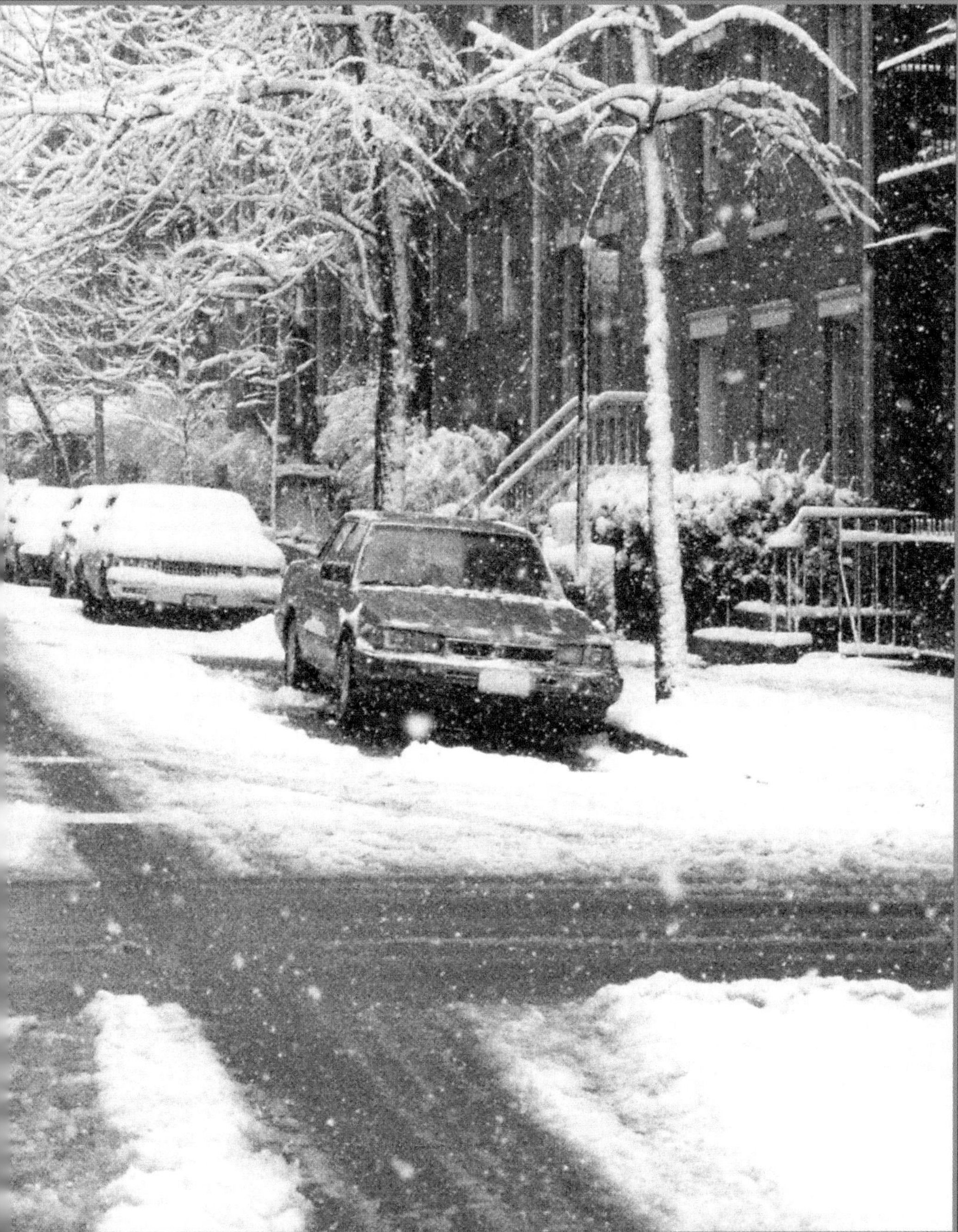

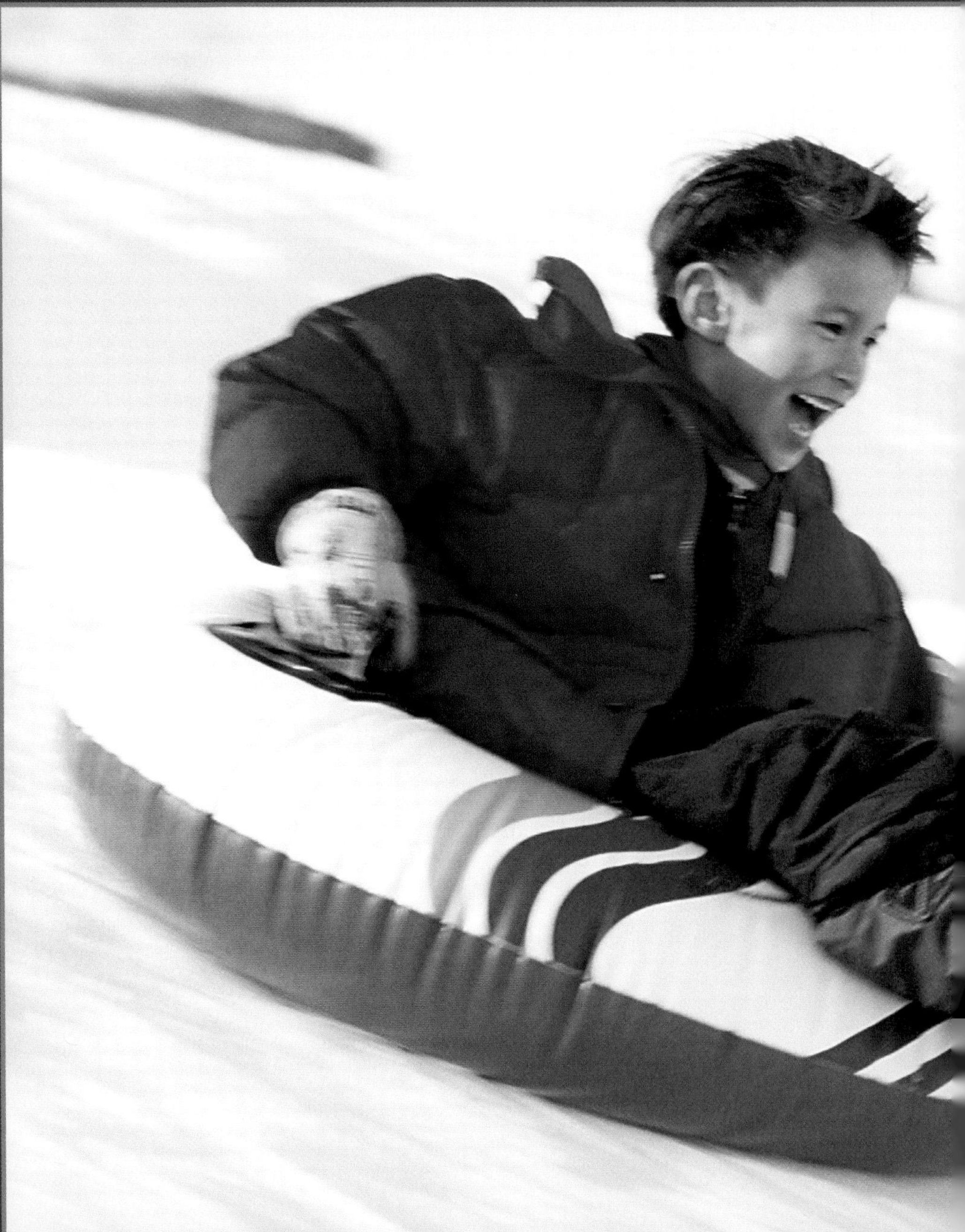

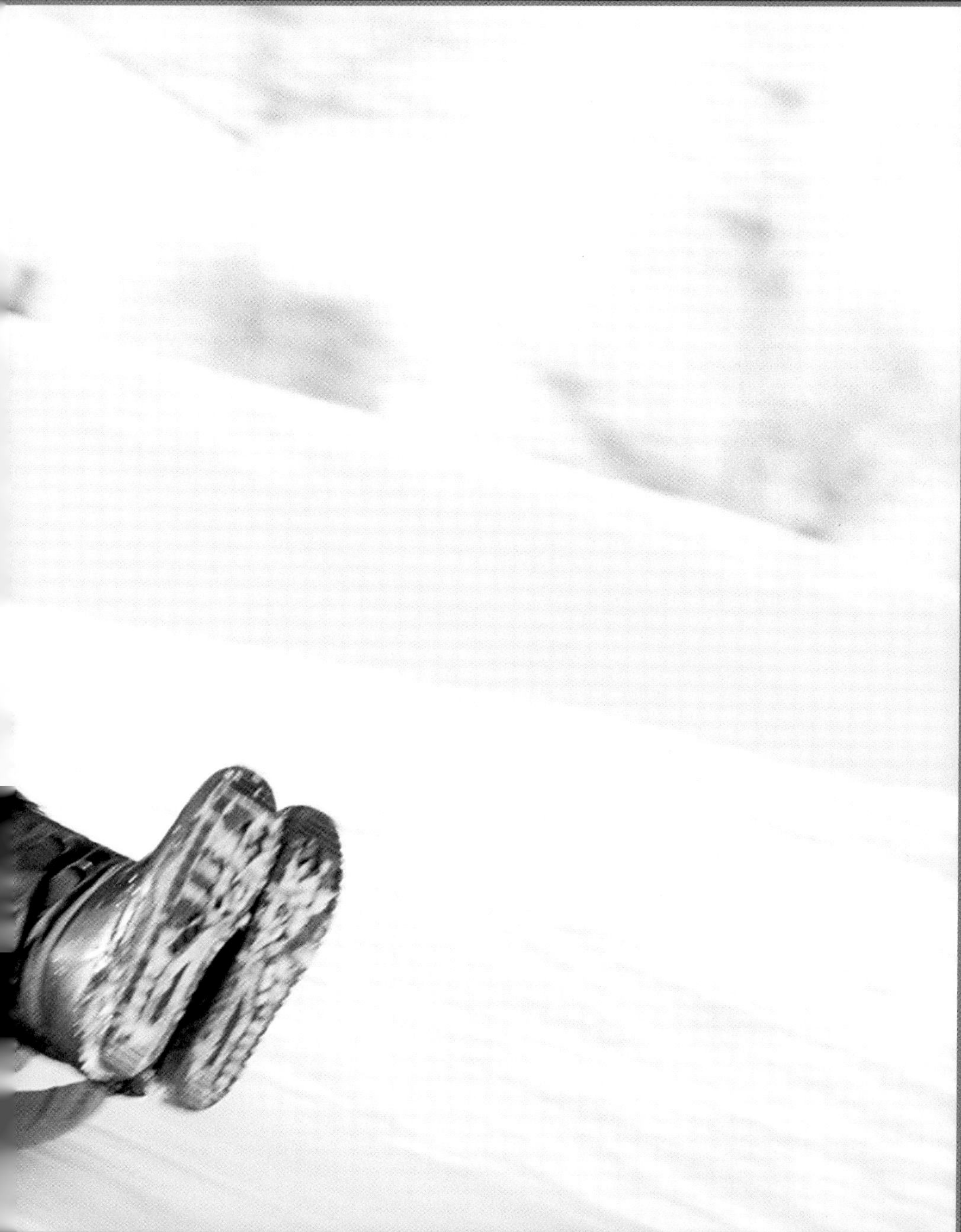

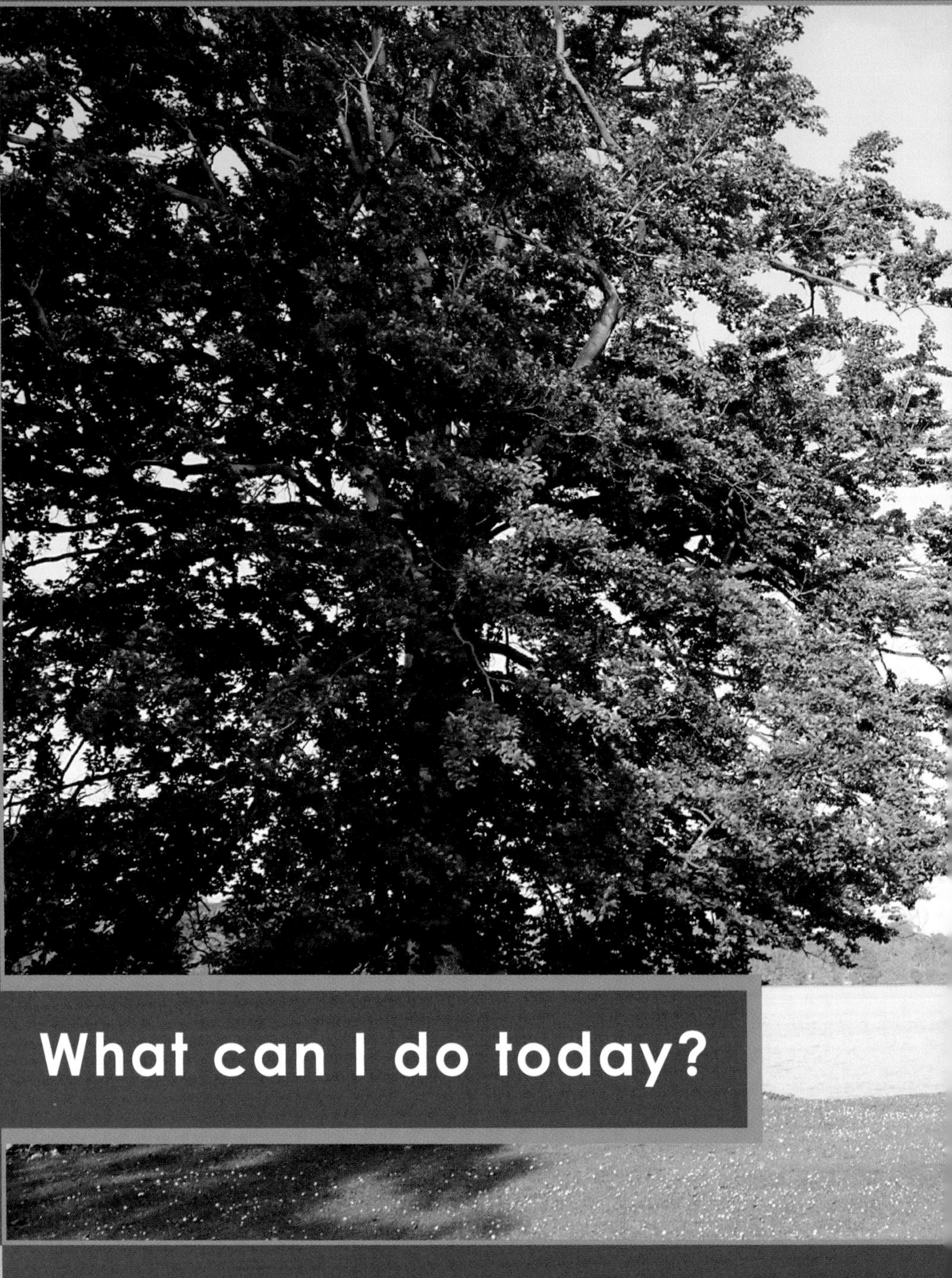

What can I do today?

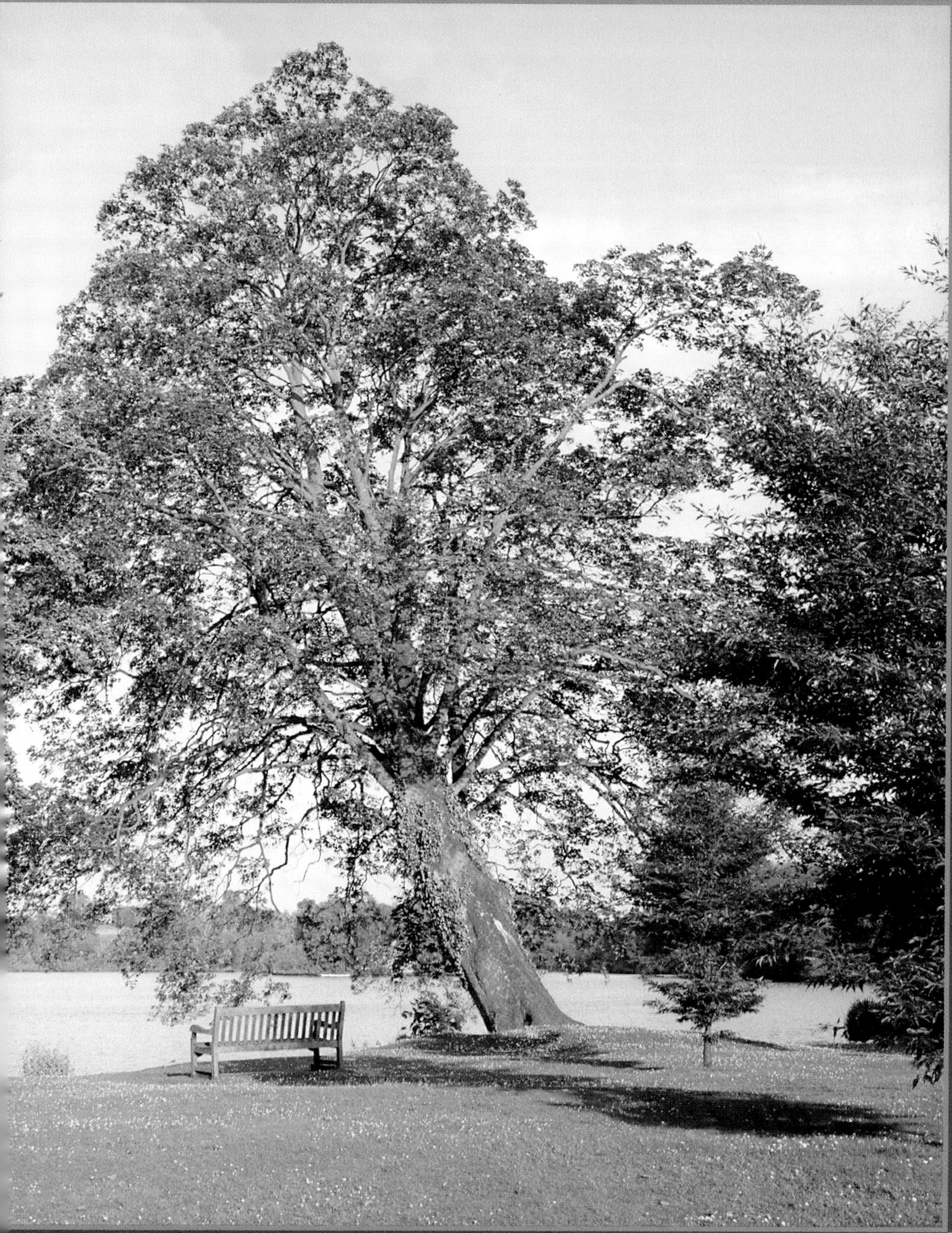

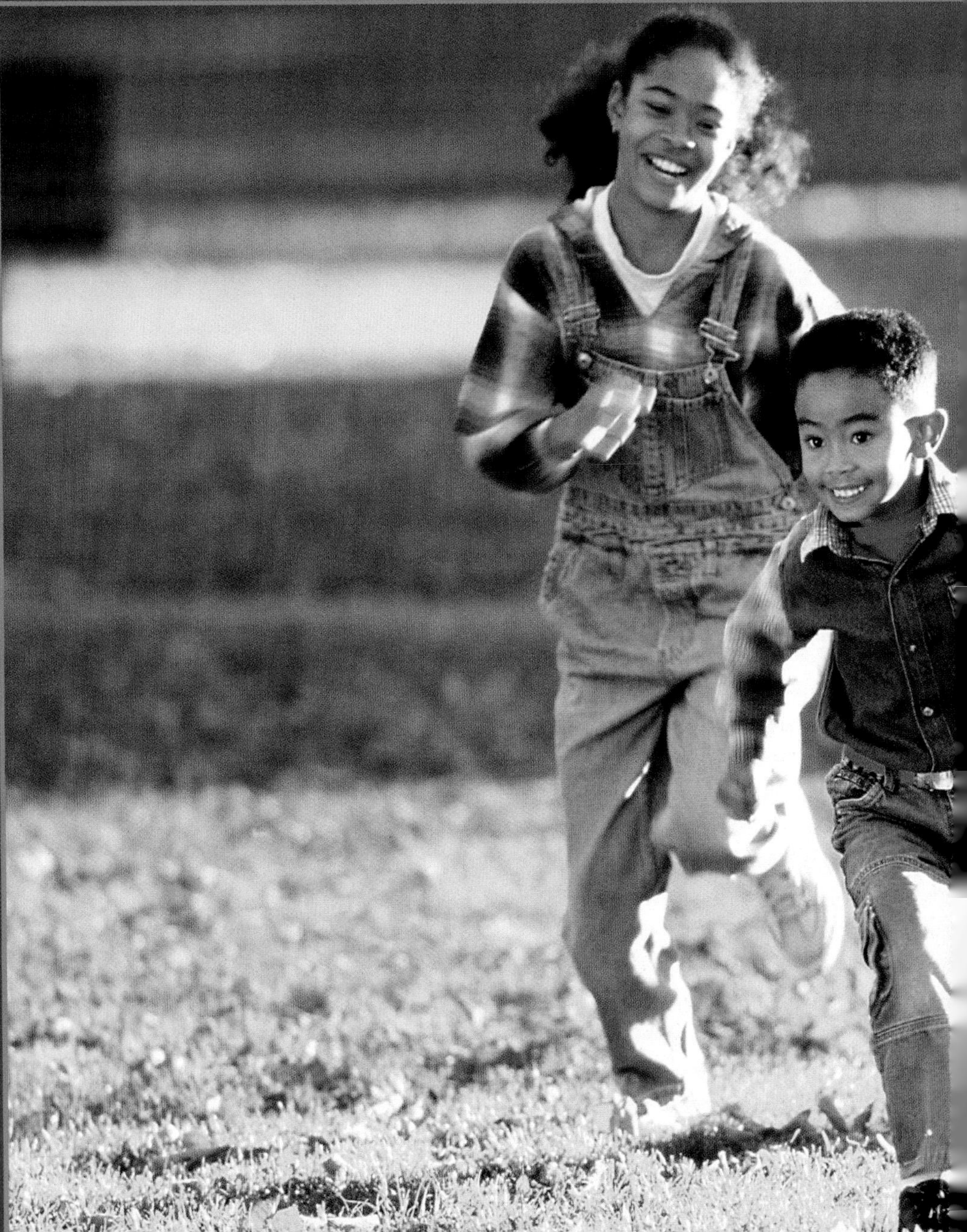

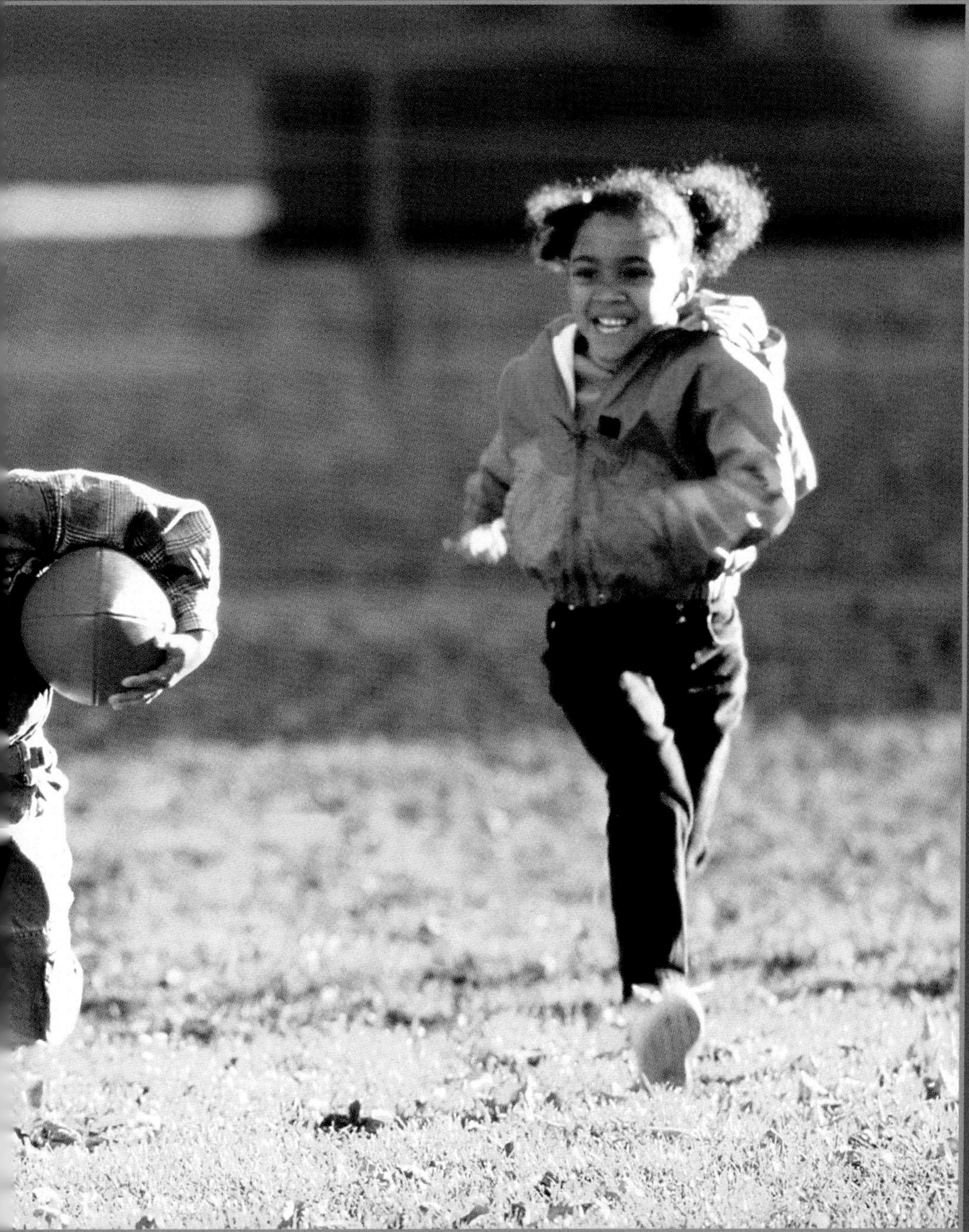

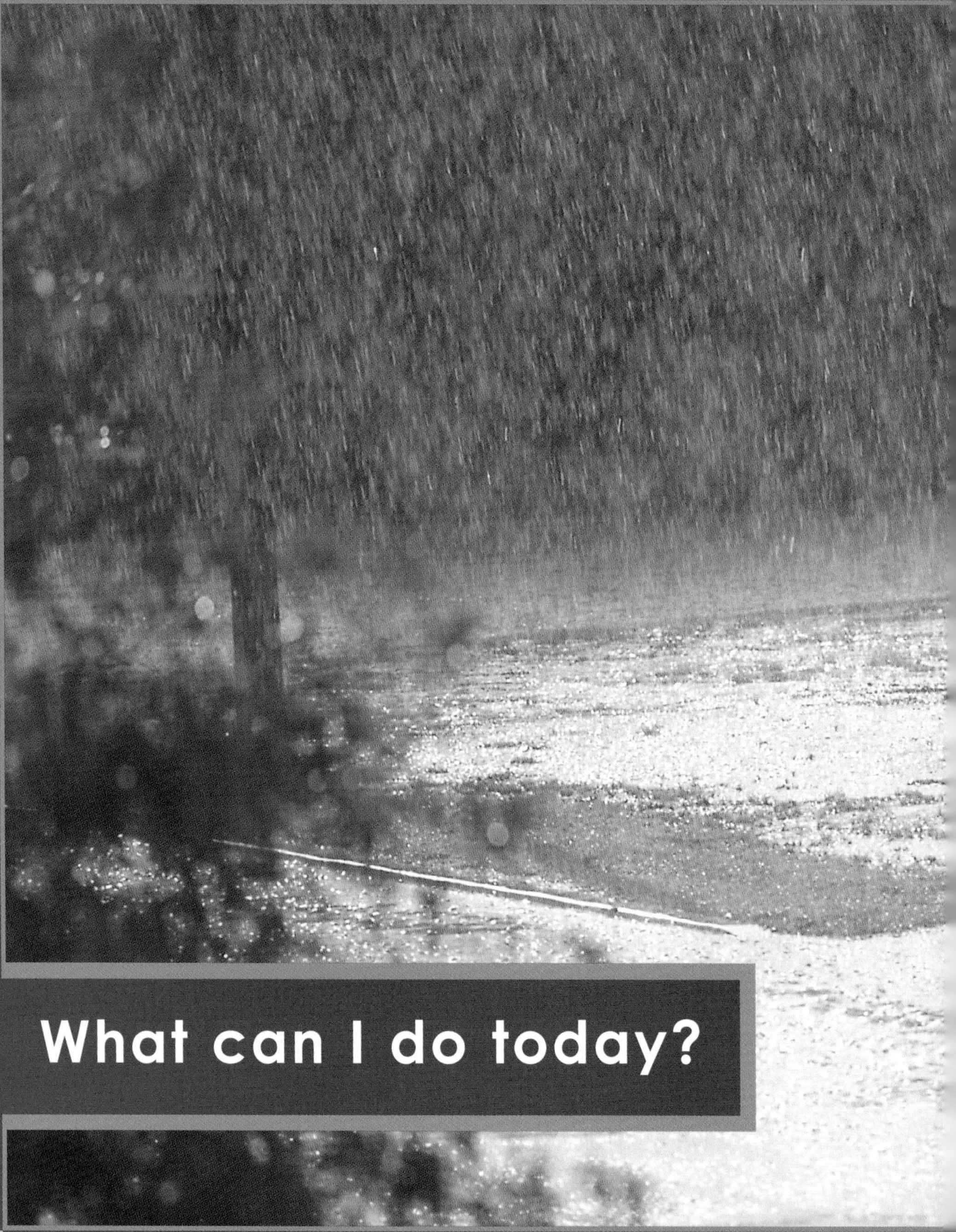

What can I do today?

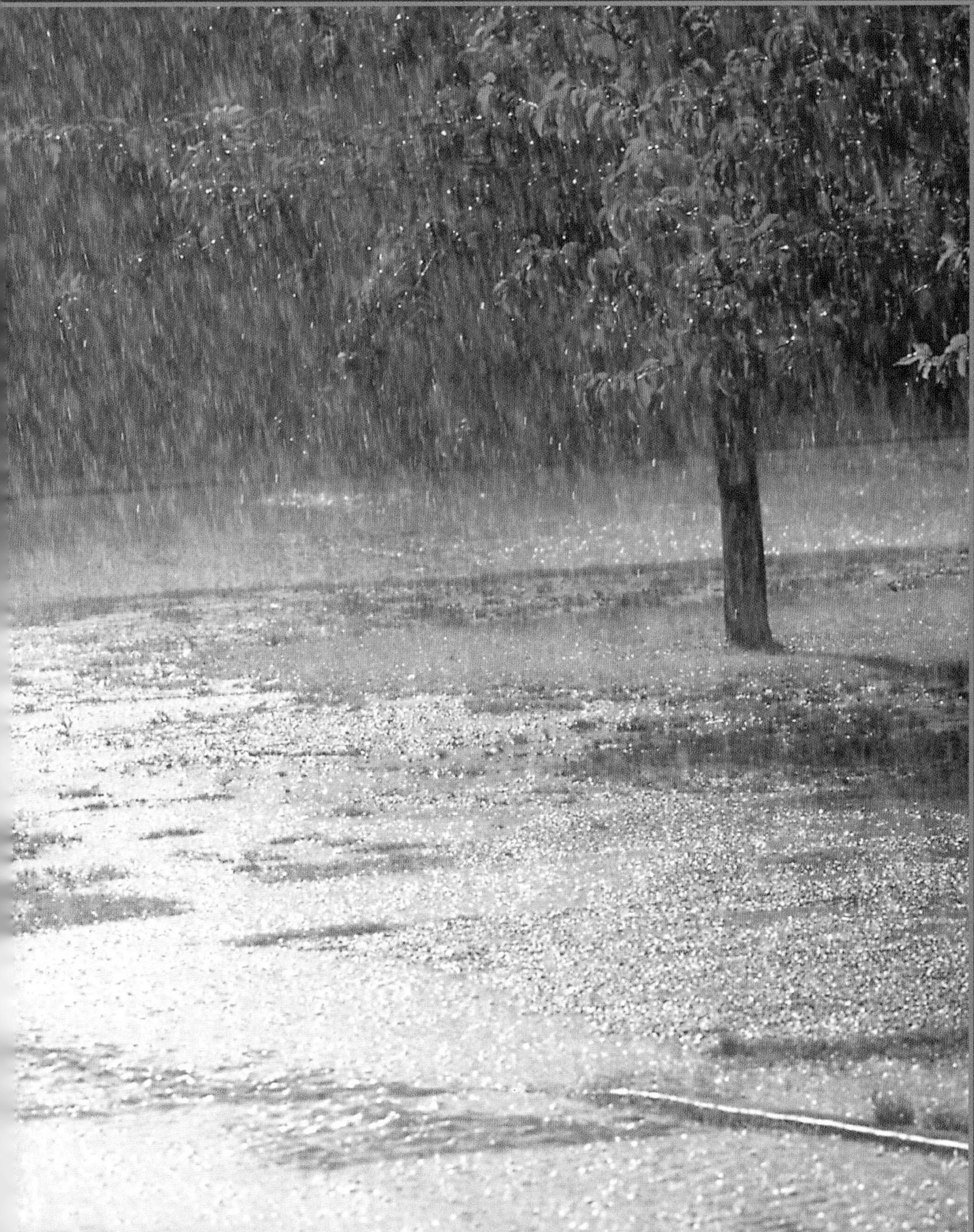

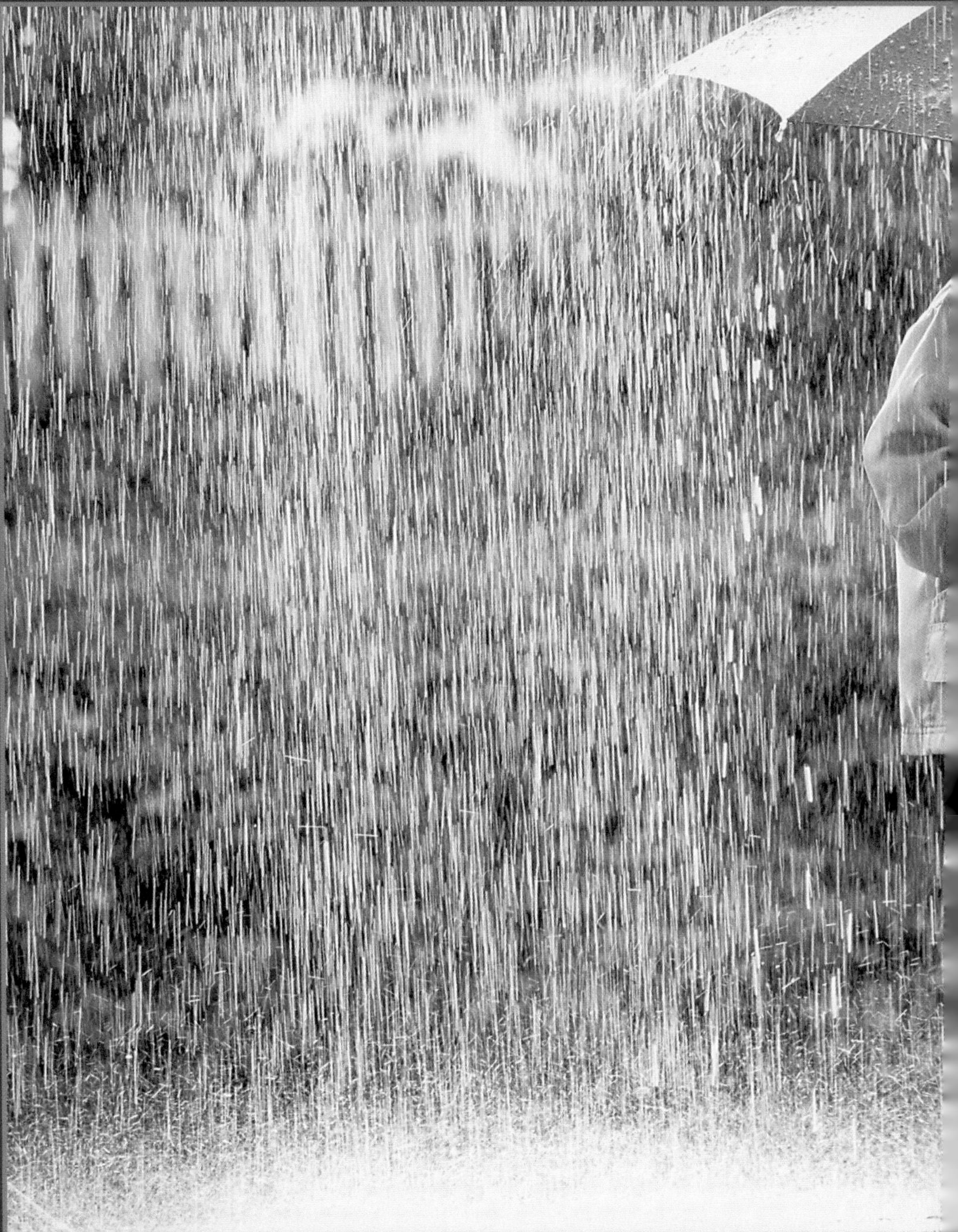

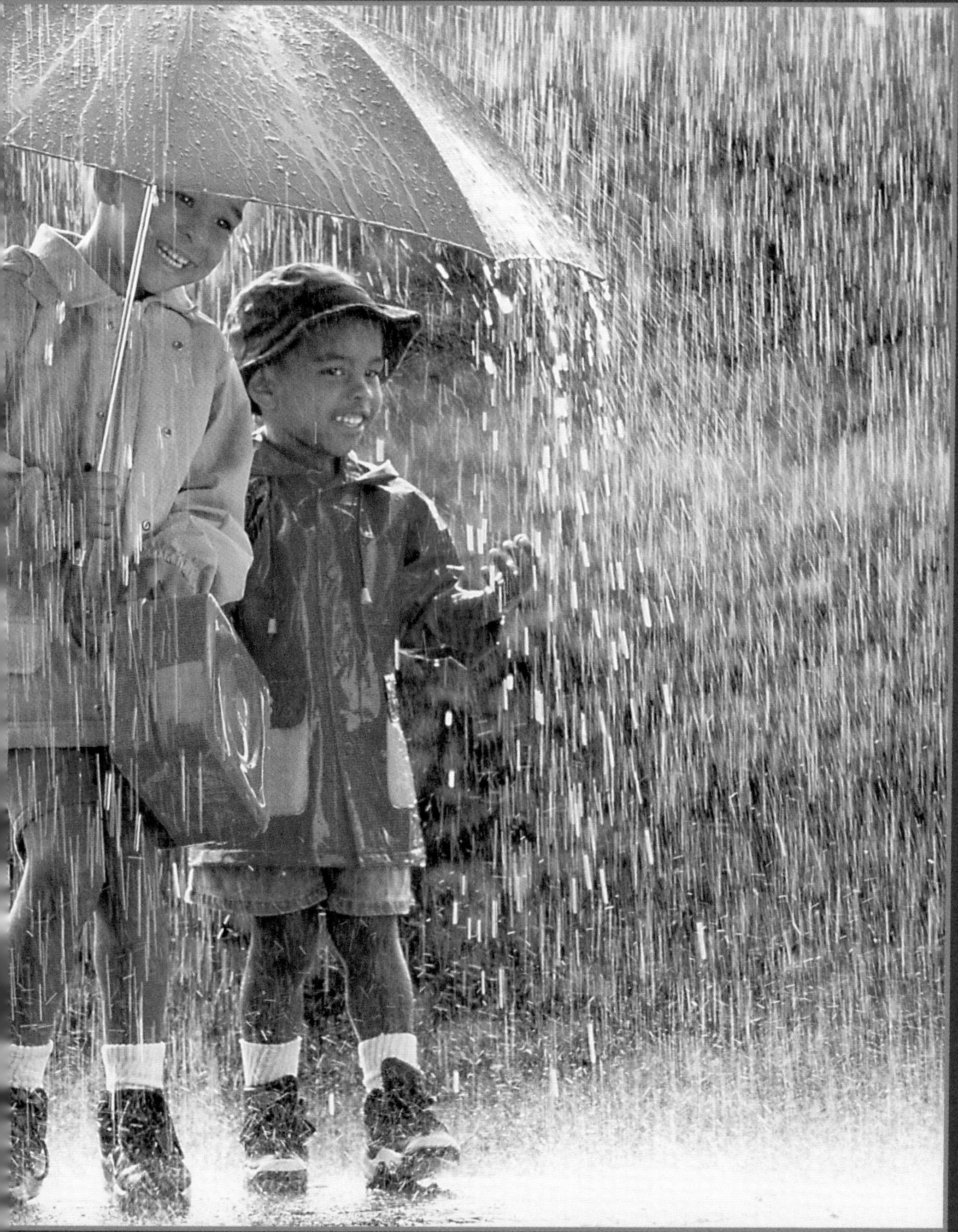

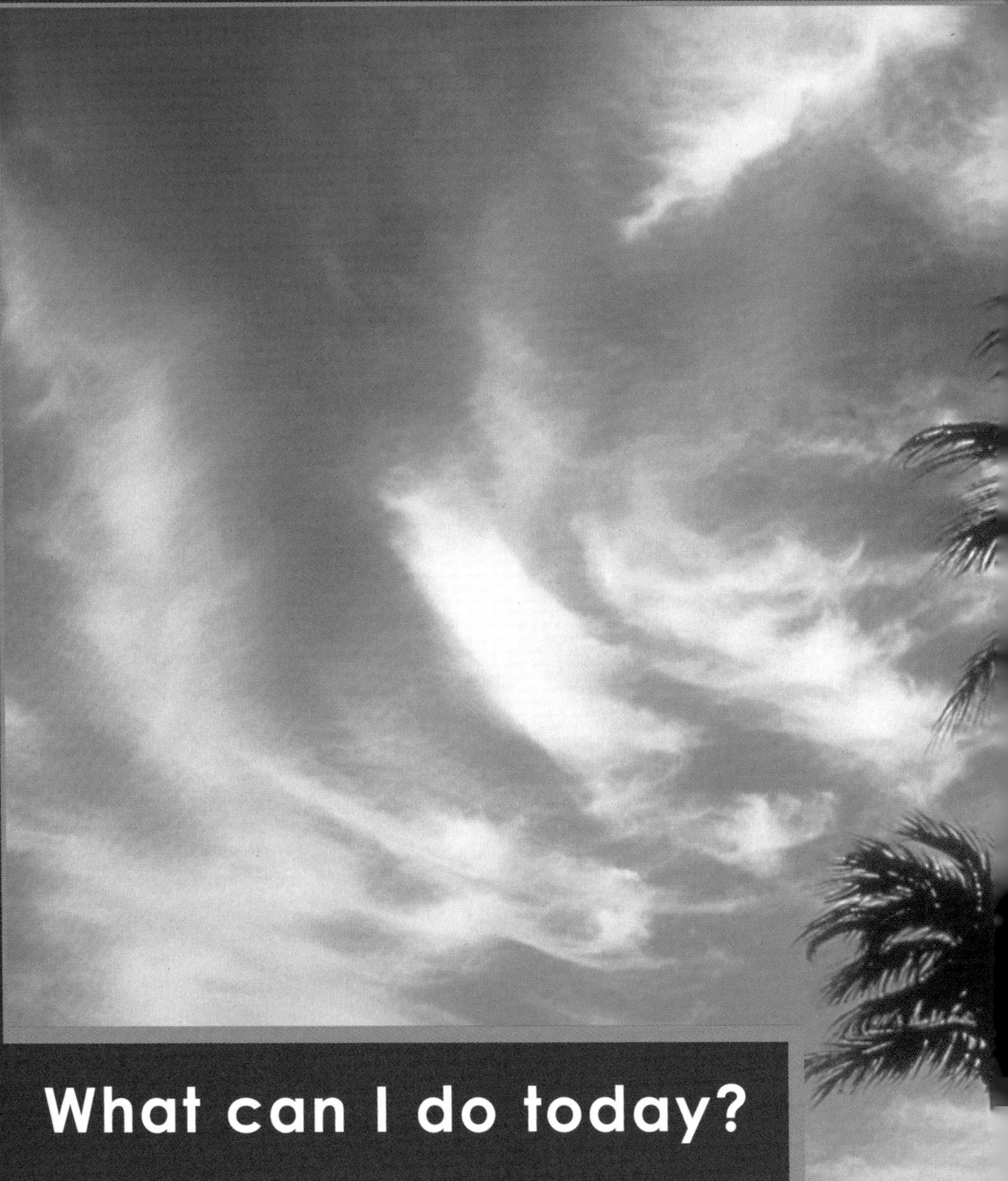

What can I do today?

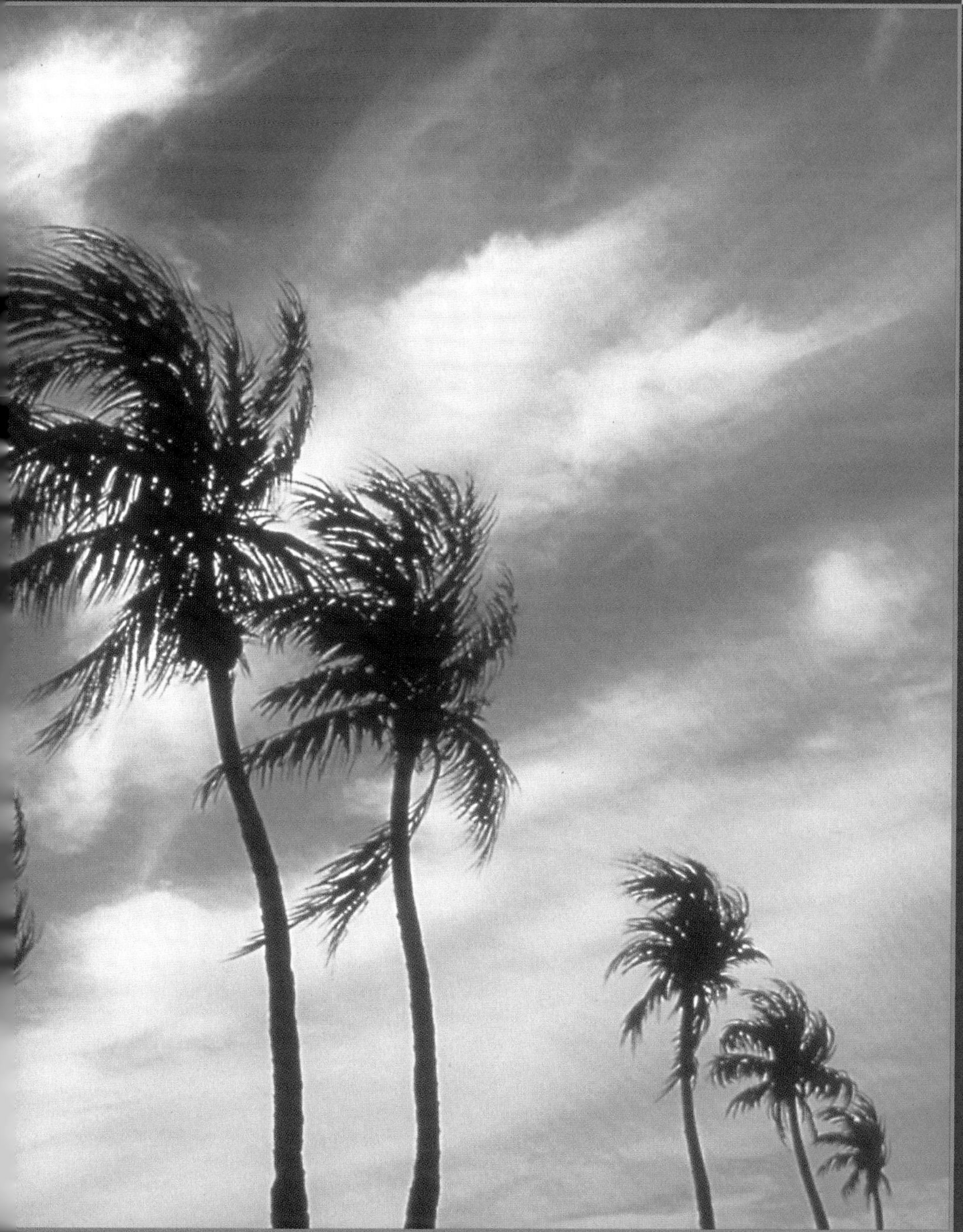

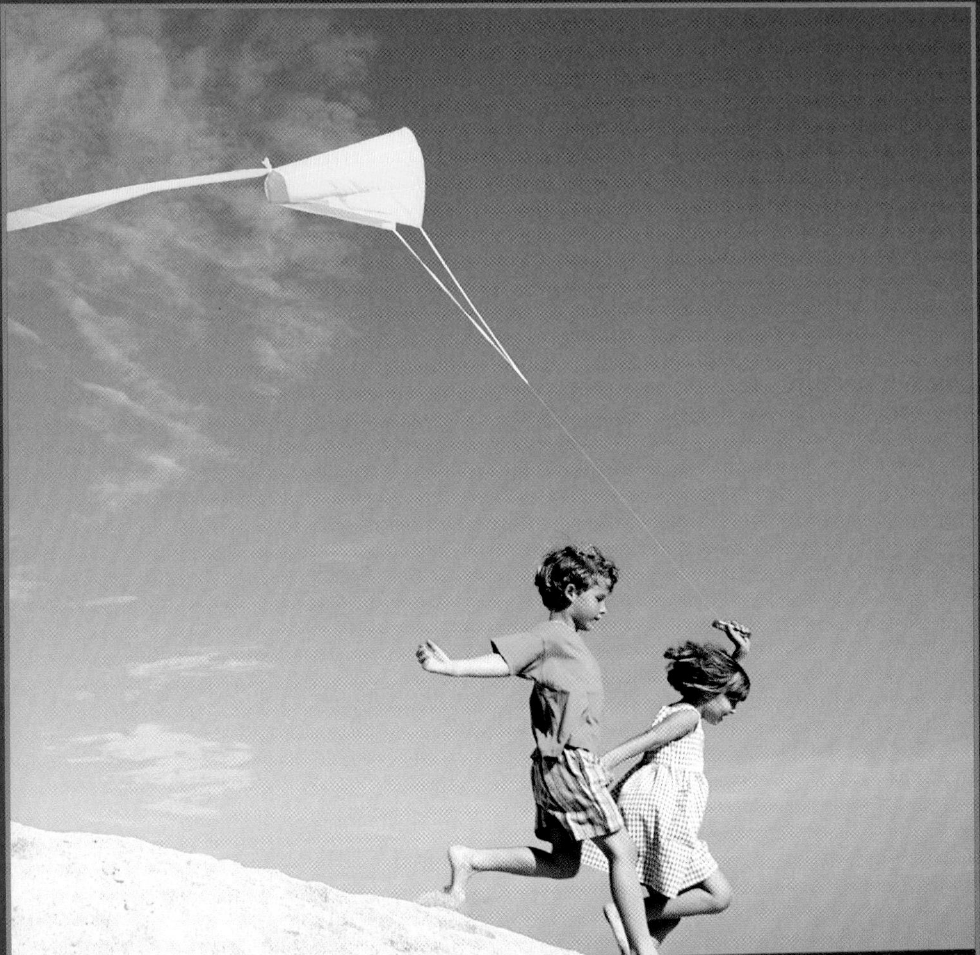